MR. PE

SHEI

Illustrated by Lilian Buchanan

BLACKIE

GLASGOW AND LONDON

ISBN 0 216 89856 0

Blackie and Son Limited
5 Fitzhardinge Street, London W1H 0DL
Bishopbriggs, Glasgow G64 2NZ

Printed in Great Britain by Robert MacLehose and Company Limited
The University Press, Glasgow

I

BAD NEWS

Mr. Penny had a farm. His farm was not very big, and he was not very rich. For Mr. Penny was old, and he had nobody to help him with the farm work.

One morning, he was sitting by the fire, and he was very upset. The King had made a new law, and it had been read out to all the farmers in the land. It went like this:

'If any man does not look after his farm, I shall take it away from him. And I shall give it to a better farmer, who will grow more oats and plums and pears and cabbages. All farms will be inspected next week.'

Mr. Penny bent closer to the fire, for it was a very cold day.

'If only my poor back were not so bent,' he said, 'I could plant the

cabbage field, and weed the leek field, and mend the hen coop. If I do not do all these things, I am sure the King will take my farm away.'

Now, Mr. Penny was a very kind man. He loved all the animals on his farm so much, that he always talked to them. And the animals were so fond of Mr. Penny that they learned to talk to him in human talk. So he went out to tell them all about it.

First of all, he went to Hob the Horse.

'Oh, Hob,' he said sadly, 'The farm is going to be taken away from me.'

'Oh, my!' said Hob. 'Poor Mr. Penny!' And he put his nose into Mr. Penny's hand.

'Poor Hob!' said Mr. Penny. 'What will happen to you? The new farmer will see that you are too old to work.'

'Well,' said Hob, 'I have a very big head. I will use it to think what to do.'

So Mr. Penny left Hob the Horse, and went across the yard. At the gate was Dandy the Dog, wagging his tail. He did not wag it very fast, for he was very old. In fact, all Mr. Penny's animals were old, and they had been with him

for a very long time. Dandy the Dog was very slow at learning things, so Mr. Penny had to tell him all about the new law very slowly. Even so, Dandy did not understand at first.

'I would like a new farmer to come here,' said Dandy. 'He may have some children and I like to play with children.'

'But if a new farmer comes, we shall all have

to go,' Mr. Penny told him. 'Then what would we do?'

Dandy was very sad when at last he understood what Mr. Penny meant.

'I will chase my tail for a while,' he said. 'That will help me to think what to do.'

Next Mr. Penny talked to Cleo the Cat. Cleo always looked as if she did not care about anybody else. But when she heard the sad news, she hissed and put out her claws and looked very angry indeed.

'I do not mind about going away from the farm,' she said. 'I can live in any place. But you poor humans, you need your houses. I shall

wash my face and paws: and as I lick, I shall think what to do.'

When Porky the Pig and Barney the Bull heard the news from Mr. Penny they were also very sad.

'The new farmer will make me into sausages!' cried Porky.

'And me into beef!' bellowed Barney.

'Oh whatever shall we do?' they all cried sadly.

2

A WAY OF HELPING

All the animals tried to think what to do. And Mr. Penny began his work very sadly. For he knew that he could not do all the jobs on the farm before the King's inspector came.

Dandy the Dog was finding it hard to think, all by himself. So he went to the other four animals and said:

'I cannot think alone. Will you all come to my part of the yard, and help me to think?'

All the animals went to the yard. They sat

down in a ring. For a long time there was no sound. Then Hob the Horse made a speech.

'For many years,' said Hob, 'we have lived on

the farm. For a long time, we have done no work. But our master, Mr. Penny, has always given us food and shelter. Even on very cold days he brings me my oats, and Cleo her milk, and Dandy his bone, and Porky his swill, and Barney his hay. Now we must work for him, and save the farm. We have learnt how to talk as humans talk. Why should we not learn to do other useful things as well?'

They all agreed that animals were just as clever as men.

'All we have to do,' said Cleo, 'is to watch what Mr. Penny does and then do the same.' And she made a list of all the things that had to be done. Then they all went to tell Mr. Penny that they were going to help him.

'You start each job,' said Hob, 'and we will finish it for you.'

Mr. Penny was afraid that they would make things worse, but he led them up to the cabbage field. He dug a hole very slowly, for his old back hurt. Then he picked up a cabbage plant, popped it into the hole, and pushed the earth back all round the plant.

'But that is easy!' said Cleo.

'It is,' said Mr. Penny, 'as long as your back does not hurt; and if the earth is soft; and if you have only a few to plant. But I must grow five hundred cabbages.'

'Well,' said Hob the Horse, 'you go back and sit by the fire. We will see what we can do.'

'Oh dear!' said Mr. Penny to himself, as he went down the path. 'They are very kind, but I fear they will spoil all my plants.'

3

CABBAGE PLANTING

When Mr. Penny had gone, the animals looked at the plants, and then at the big field, and then at each other.

'Go on,' said Porky the Pig. 'Go on, Hob. You said we could do it. Now you show us what we have to do.'

Hob was not sure that he could, but Barney had an idea.

'I am a strong bull,' he said in his deep voice. 'I will walk up and down the field. I shall follow my horns, so that I walk in a straight line. And I will stamp hard, every time I put down my left back hoof. That will break the hard earth.'

'And I will follow you,' said Dandy the Dog. 'Once the earth is loose, I can make a hole with my paws. I will pretend that there is a big bone hidden. Then it will be like a game.'

'We have begun well,' said Hob. 'What about you, Porky? What can you do to help Mr. Penny?'

'I am not very pretty,' said Porky, 'but I have a clever nose. I can use it to push each plant into the hole once Dandy has dug it.'

'Splendid, Porky!' said Hob. 'That is just what we need. Now what else has to be done?'

'Who can carry the cabbage plants to the holes?' asked Barney. 'None of us has hands like humans.'

'I am really too lady-like for such work,' said Cleo the Cat. 'But I have a strong mouth. I used to carry my kittens in it. It is also a soft mouth. So I can pick up the little plants and lay one beside each hole. I shall not hurt them any more than I hurt my kittens.'

'Good,' said Hob. 'Now, when Barney the Bull has loosened the earth: and Dandy the Dog has made a hole: and Cleo the Cat has laid a plant by the hole: and Porky the Pig has pushed the plant into the hole: I shall come along after you all, and push the earth all around the plant, just as Mr. Penny did.

'I'm sure we can do the work properly. And there are five of us so that we should be able to finish it ever so much more quickly than Mr. Penny.'

So they set to work. At first it was great fun. They followed one another slowly along the rows. Barney stamped and Dandy dug and Cleo carried and Porky pushed and Hob finished all the work off.

But it was a very big field, and five hundred is a great number of plants to put in. Little by little the animals began to get a little cross and tired.

'Ha, ha!' purred Cleo. 'Doesn't Porky look funny? His nose is all muddy.'

'It is very sore, too,' cried Porky. But he went on pushing each plant into its hole!

'My left back hoof is sore too,' said Barney. 'It's this hard ground that's hurting it.' But, though he grumbled, he plodded on. One, two, three—*wallop!* One, two, three—*wallop!*

'I cannot find any bones,' said Dandy. 'This isn't like a game any more.' But he went on making the holes until his paws hurt him.

'If only I were not so big,' said Hob. 'It is very hard to push the earth round these little plants with my big hooves, and stamp it down. I nearly tread on the plants every time and it does worry me a lot. Whatever would Mr. Penny say if I spoiled all his cabbage plants with my clumsy hooves?'

Cleo said nothing. She

had just carried the last plant to its hole. Now she ran back to the farm house to ask Mr. Penny to come and see. And what do you think he saw?

Under the setting sun, Dandy lay licking his paws. Porky was wiping his snout in some cool, wet grass. Hob was lying on his back with his legs in the air. Barney was standing in the stream at the end of the field, to make his left back hoof feel better.

And there were five hundred happy little cabbage plants, standing like rows of soldiers, up and down the field.

Mr. Penny did not

know what to say. So he just said, 'Thank you, Hob, Cleo, Dandy, Barney and Porky, very much,' and they all went home to supper.

4

THE KING'S INSPECTOR

The next day, and for three more days, they worked in the same way. Always they found that they were able to do the work, if Mr. Penny showed them how. Soon the farm looked just as a farm should.

But there was still one more day before the King's inspector was to come. So Mr. Penny found some paint. Swish, swosh, swush, went the tails of Barney and Hob. And soon the fence, the hen-house, the pig-sty and the stable were all painted.

The next day, they all stood at the gate waiting to see the King's inspector. They were all sure that he would say that Mr. Penny's farm was well looked after. All the same, they were just a little worried.

Then a man rode up at great speed.

'Are you Mr. Penny?' he said, all out of breath.

'Yes, sir, I am,' said Mr. Penny.

'I have come from the King. The King now thinks that his law was not a very good law, so he has torn it up. There will not be an inspection after all.' And away he rode.

'Well!' said Mr. Penny.

'Well!' said the animals all together. And they looked rather cross.

But Hob was very wise. He said to them all:

'The King has changed his mind once. Perhaps

he will change it again. So let us always help Mr. Penny. Then he will always be ready for the King's inspector.'

And they did.